What does
SANTA
have for
BREAKFAST?

A Seasonal Assortment
of Puzzles and Games

BY JIM GALLAGHER &
HELENE HOVANEC

A TRUMPET CLUB ORIGINAL BOOK

ISBN: 0-590-10710-0

Copyright © 1997 by Jim Gallagher & Helene Hovanec.
All rights reserved. Published by Scholastic Inc.
TRUMPET and the TRUMPET logo are registered
trademarks of Scholastic Inc.

12   0 12/0

Printed in the U.S.A.

First Scholastic printing, December 1997

THE GAME OF THE NAME

Only one box has all the correct letters of **SANTA CLAUS**. Which one is it?

1.
ATLNS
LUSCA

2.
ATNAL
SUCLU

3.
CLASU
ASTNS

4.
AAUNS
LTCAC

5.
NUTLA
CSSNA

6.
ACSAN
TULAS

7.
SAATA
SUACL

8.
ASNLC
TAUST

HOWDY!

Follow the directions below to cross off the letters described in each clue and you'll answer this riddle:

HOW DO ANGELS GREET EACH OTHER?

1. Cross off every letter that comes after "S" in the alphabet.

2. Cross off every "E" and "I."

3. Cross off every "M" and "N."

4. Place the remaining letters in the spaces below. Work from left to right and top to bottom.

X	E	M	W	E	T	E	W
Y	Z	X	M	T	I	M	X
Z	H	E	N	I	X	I	E
I	V	U	X	M	I	X	Y
U	N	M	N	V	W	A	Z
X	M	I	X	E	M	Y	U
M	Z	N	L	T	I	N	W
I	N	X	I	M	U	M	O

__ __ __ __ __

MAKING CONNECTIONS #1

Connect the dots from 1 to 65 to find out what someone could be doing on December 24th.

SCRAMBLER

Unscramble the letters of each word below to find a riddle and its answer.

HWY   SNDE'TO   IANST
COLAHNSI   VAHES?

VRYEE   MEIT   EH   RSEIT
EH   SCINK   FILMSHE.

FIND THE TWINS #1

Find the two identical ornaments.

PUN FUN

Use the code on this page to read a riddle and its answer on the next page.

A = @		M = •
B = ¶		N = #
C = $		O = £
D = &		P = *
E = Δ		R = 🍎
H = +		S = √
I = ¤		T = ‡
J = ¢		U = ®
L = (		W = ©
Y = %		

© + %　　　& £ Δ √

* Δ @ # ® ‡　　¶ ® ‡ ‡ Δ

+ @ ‡ Δ　　$ + ¤ √ ‡ • @ √ ?

¶ Δ $ @ ® √ Δ　　' ‡ ¤ √

‡ + Δ　　√ Δ @ √ £ #

‡ £　　¶ Δ　　¢ Δ ((% .

9

OPPOSITE DISTRACTION

The name of a Christmas celebrity is hidden here. Fill the grid with words that are the **OPPOSITES** of the clues. Be sure to start writing each word in a numbered box. Some words start in the middle row and some words end in the middle row. When all the boxes are filled in, you'll find this celebrity.

1. ALWAYS
2. OVER
3. HATED
4. YOUNGER

5. BIG
6. FANCY
7. THROW

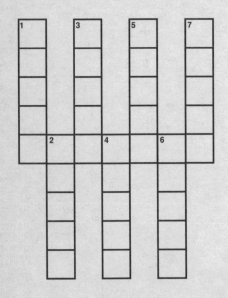

SPELLING LINES #1

After you recognize each thing in the top boxes, write the first letter of its name in the box at the other end of the line. Then read the letters across to spell the name of a well-known traveler.

MISSING PERSON

One of the holiday shoppers on this page is not on the opposite page. Which person is missing?

HA! HA!

Find a riddle and its answer by changing each letter to the one that comes just before it in the alphabet.

XIBU HPFT "IP, IP, IP, QMPQ"?

TBOUB DMBVT MBVHIJOH IJT

IFBE PGG.

A-MAZE #1

Make a path through this maze for Santa to get from the roof to the stockings.

SEASON'S GREETINGS

Many workers advertise their services or products through holiday cards. Match each card with the worker who would send it to his or her customers.

THE REAL SANTA

Fill in the numbered spaces below with the letters indicated and answer this riddle:

WHAT DOES SANTA DO AFTER CHRISTMAS?

A = 4, 6, 14, 17, 21
E = 2, 9, 26, 29
F = 5
H = 1, 12, 24, 27
L = 15
M = 8
O = 13, 25, 28
R = 7, 10
S = 3, 19, 20, 23
W = 11, 16
Y = 18, 22

___ ___ ___ , ___   ___ ___ ___ ___ ___ ___
1   2   3   4   5   6   7   8   9   10

___ ___ ___   ___ ___ ___ ___ ___ ___   ___ ___ ___ ___ ,
11 12 13   14 15 16 17 18 19   20 21 22 23

" ___ ___ ___   ___ ___ ___ . "
24 25 26   27 28 29

MISSING PIECE #1

Which piece was removed from the picture?

OH, DEER!

Uh-oh! Someone got into Santa's yard and took away a piece of each reindeer. You can get Santa's team ready for the big night by placing one of the two-letter pieces from the right column into each empty space in the left column.

C _ _ I D	AN
R U _ _ L P H	AS
P R A N C _ _	DO
B L _ _ Z E N	EN
D _ _ N E R	ER
D _ _ H E R	IT
V I X _ _	ME
C O _ _ T	ON
D _ _ C E R	UP

BOXED OUT #1

Each small picture on the bottom of the page is part of the large picture on top. Can you locate each one by number and letter?

HOLIDAY FEAST

Your mouth will water as you put each delicious food into the one spot in the grid where it belongs. To start, put the only ten-letter word in the only ten-letter space.

THREE LETTERS
HAM
PIE

FOUR LETTERS
BEEF
CAKE
DUCK
SOUP
YAMS

FIVE LETTERS
BREAD
FRUIT
PUNCH
SALAD

SIX LETTERS
EGGNOG
TURKEY

SEVEN LETTERS
CHICKEN
COOKIES

EIGHT LETTERS
POTATOES
STUFFING

TEN LETTERS
APPLESAUCE

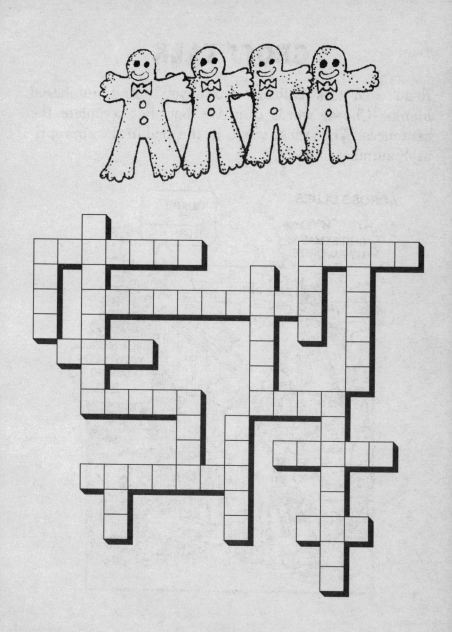

CROSS TALK

Read each talk balloon, where you'll find numbered blanks. Choose words from the list that complete the sentences. Write those words in the grid in the appropriately numbered spots.

ACROSS CLUES

DOWN CLUES

WORD LIST

ARTIST
CATCH
CUP
DECORATED
DINNER
HERE
HOLIDAY
PAPER
PLAY
PRETTY

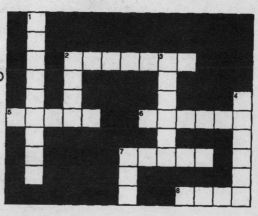

25

SITE-SEEING

Fill in the blank space to make the name of a spot you'd find on a map. Then read **DOWN** the column to find Santa's site.

```
CONTI_ENT
     _CEAN
COUNT_Y
  STA_E
     _ILL

     _RAIRIE
   M_UNTAIN
  IS_AND
   D_SERT
```

HIDDEN WORDS

There are five Christmas words hidden in this picture. Can you find each one?

RIDDLE READ

A riddle and its answer are written here. The words are in the correct order, but the spacing is wrong. Can you read it?

INW HA T

MO VI ED

OE S SAN

TAME E TAL

IE NS? CL

AUS EN CO

UN TERS

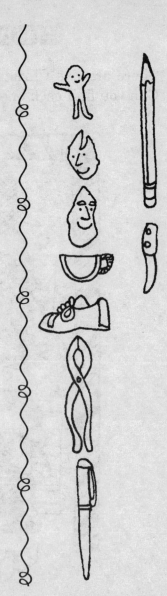

LOST AND FOUND

Look at the nine small pictures on the right side of the opposite page. Each one is hidden somewhere in this big picture. Can you find and circle each one?

JUST JOKING

Look at the words on the opposite page and cross off the groups described below. When you're finished, read the remaining words from left to right and top to bottom to find the answer to this riddle:

WHAT DID ADAM SAY ON DECEMBER 24TH?

1. Cross off 5 colors.

2. Cross off 5 words that rhyme with RARE.

3. Cross off 5 U.S. cities

4. Cross off 2 types of cars.

5. Cross off 3 lunch foods.

6. Cross off 2 rooms in a house.

7. Cross off 3 things to read.

DARE   BOSTON   GREEN   PIZZA   BOOK

HAMBURGER   IT'S   KITCHEN   CARE

RICHMOND   MARE   BLUE

BEDROOM   TULSA

YELLOW   PARE   DALLAS   CHRISTMAS

SEDAN   PURPLE   SANDWICH   FARE   RENO

NEWSPAPER   RED   EVE   DIARY

CONVERTIBLE

BOXED OUT #2

Each small picture on the opposite page is part of the large picture on this page. Can you locate each one by number and letter?

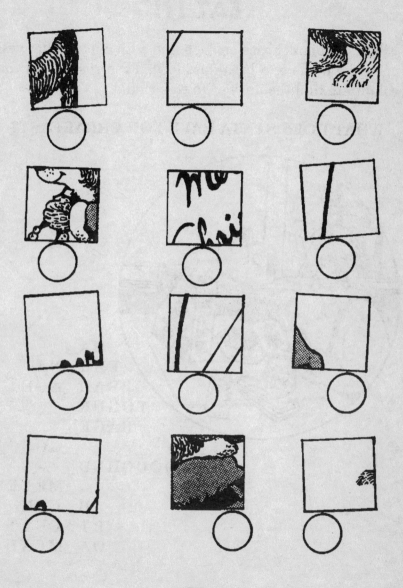

EAT IT!

Fill in the blank space on each line with a letter that will spell the name of a breakfast food. Then read down the column to find the answer to this riddle:

WHAT DOES SANTA HAVE FOR BREAKFAST?

HA__

FAR__NA

SAU__AGE

YOGUR__

BAGE__

__GGS

DOUGHNU__

__MELET

B__CON

BI__CUIT

OA__MEAL

STORY LINE

Number the boxes from 1 to 5 to make a story without words.

OOPS!

Fill in the blank space on each line with a letter that will spell the name of something Santa might have in his bag. Then read down the column to find the answer to this riddle:

WHAT DO YOU CALL A CLUMSY SANTA?

         TR_IN

         _KATES
         W_GON
CLOTHI_G
         WA_CH
         R_DIO

         BOO_
   BICYC_E
     COMP_TER
         _RUCK
     PUZ_LE

SPELLING LINES #2

After you recognize each thing in the top boxes, write the first letter of its name in the box at the other end of the line. Then read the letters across to spell the name of a heavenly creature.

SOME SONG!

In the grid on the next page, find and circle each of the fourteen musical instruments listed below. Look forward, backward, up, down, and diagonally. **VIOLIN** is circled to start you off. When you've circled all the words, write the **UNUSED** letters from the grid in the blank spaces at the bottom of the opposite page. Go in order from left to right and top to bottom, and you'll answer this riddle:

WHAT DO MONSTERS SING AT CHRISTMAS?

DRUM
FIDDLE
FLUTE
GUITAR
HORN
KAZOO
LYRE
OBOE
ORGAN
PIANO
TROMBONE
TRUMPET
~~VIOLIN~~
XYLOPHONE

T	R	O	M	B	O	N	E	V	E
E	R	M	D	E	C	O	R	I	N
T	G	U	I	T	A	R	K	O	O
U	T	R	M	H	E	G	H	L	H
L	P	D	A	P	L	A	L	I	P
F	I	D	D	L	E	N	S	N	O
W	A	I	T	H	P	T	O	B	L
I	N	S	K	A	Z	O	O	O	Y
N	O	I	L	Y	R	E	V	Y	X

RIDDLE ANSWER: _ _ _ _ _ _ _

_ _ _ _ _ _ _ _ _

_ _ _ _ _ _ _ _ _

SOME PLACE!

Put each word into the grid in alphabetical order. Then read down one of the columns to find a place where Santa spends a lot of time.

WIPERS
HURLED
BEWARE
SCHEME
PUSHED
FROZEN
TROLLS
LIKING

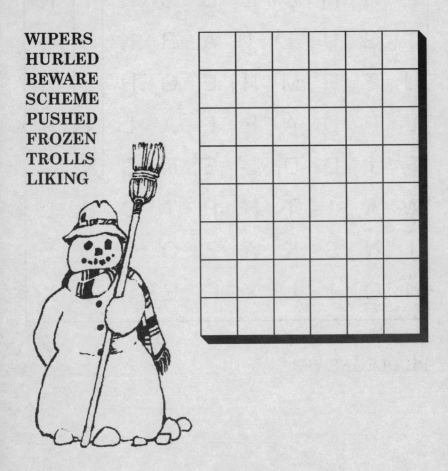

TEST YOUR MEMORY

Look at this page for one minute. Then turn to the next page and answer the questions. No fair peeking!

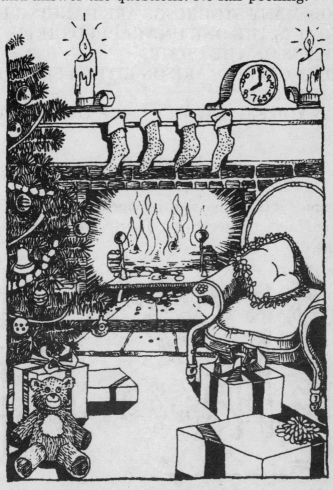

QUESTIONS

1. WHAT TIME IS IT?
2. IS THERE A FIRE IN THE FIREPLACE?
3. HOW MANY STOCKINGS ARE HANGING UP?
4. WHAT IS THE ONE UNWRAPPED GIFT?
5. WHAT'S ON THE CHAIR?
6. WHAT OBJECTS ARE ON EITHER SIDE OF THE CLOCK?
7. CAN YOU SEE THE WHOLE CHRISTMAS TREE?

REBUS

Add and subtract the pictures and letters in the order given to find a mystery word. Then write the word on the blanks.

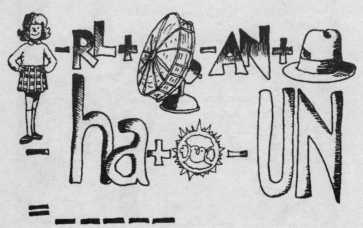

SOME DIFFERENCE

Find five differences between these two Santas.

A-MAZE #2

Draw a path for the Christmas tree buyer to leave the forest.

SIGN OF THE TIMES

Color each space that has a dark circle (·) and you'll find a seasonal sign.

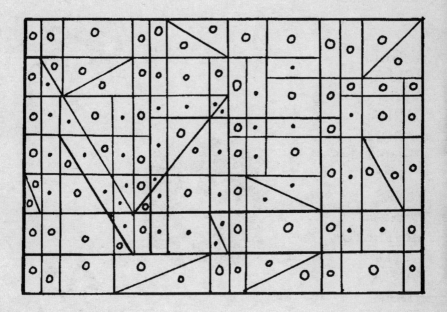

'TIS THE SEASON

In the grid on the next page, find and circle each of the eighteen seasonal words listed below. Look forward, backward, up, down, and diagonally. **HOLLY** is circled to start you off.

ANGEL
BELLS
BOWS
CARDS
CAROLS
CHRISTMAS
GIFTS
ELVES
~~HOLLY~~
MISTLETOE
PARTY
SANTA
STARS
STOCKINGS
TINSEL
TOYS
TREE
WREATH

M	J	C	A	R	O	L	S	K	D
I	X	A	J	G	I	F	T	S	Z
S	W	R	L	E	G	N	A	Z	S
T	R	D	V	S	E	M	R	Q	W
L	E	S	N	I	T	R	S	N	O
E	A	W	Z	S	A	N	T	A	B
T	T	Y	I	E	L	V	E	S	E
O	H	R	J	P	A	R	T	Y	L
E	H	O	L	L	Y	M	Q	O	L
C	S	G	N	I	K	C	O	T	S

DRAW IT!

You can be an artist and create a Christmas picture if you follow these directions:

Find box A1 on the opposite page and copy it into box A1 on this page.

Then copy box A2 from the opposite page into box A2 on this page.

Continue doing this until you've copied all the boxes. Show your finished picture to a friend!

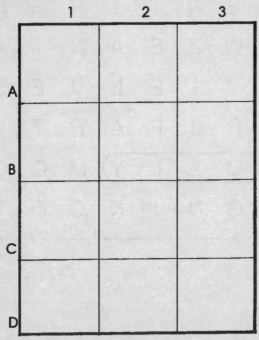

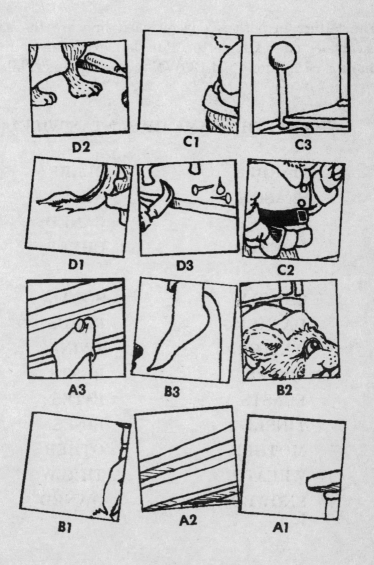

D2

C1

C3

D1

D3

C2

A3

B3

B2

B1

A2

A1

49

MRS. CLAUS

The letters in both words on each line are the same except for one extra letter. Put that extra letter in the blank space. Then read **DOWN** to answer this riddle:

WHAT IS THE NAME OF SANTA'S WIFE?

MARBLE	__	BLARE
SEASON	__	NOSES
DANCER	__	CANED
CHEERY	__	CHEER
CAROLS	__	SOLAR
DASHER	__	READS
WINTER	__	TWINE
SISTER	__	RESTS
FEASTS	__	FATES
TINSEL	__	LINES
MOTHER	__	OTHER
WREATH	__	THREW
SNOWED	__	OWNED

MAKING CONNECTIONS #2

Connect the dots from 1 to 60 to find out what someone could be doing on December 26th.

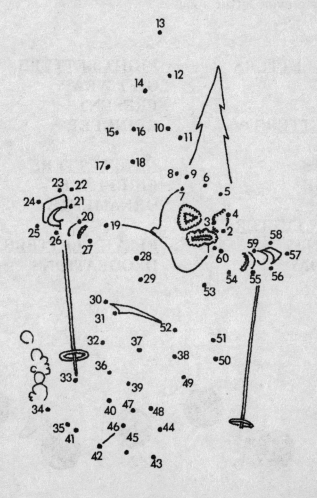

HOLIDAY FILL

Each word will fit into just one spot in the grid on the opposite page. To start, put the only eleven-letter word in the only eleven-letter space.

FOUR LETTERS
SNOW

SIX LETTERS
FAMILY
LIGHTS
SLEIGH

SEVEN LETTERS
CHIMNEY
HOLIDAY

EIGHT LETTERS
GIFT WRAP
PRESENTS
REINDEER

NINE LETTERS
FIREPLACE
ORNAMENTS

ELEVEN LETTERS
DECORATIONS

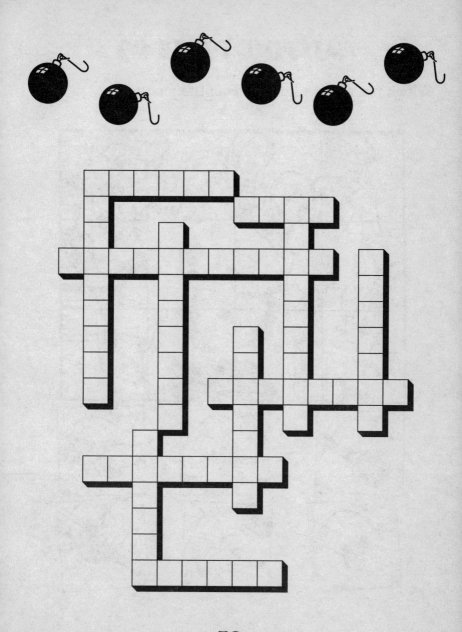

MISSING PIECE #2

Which piece was removed from the picture?

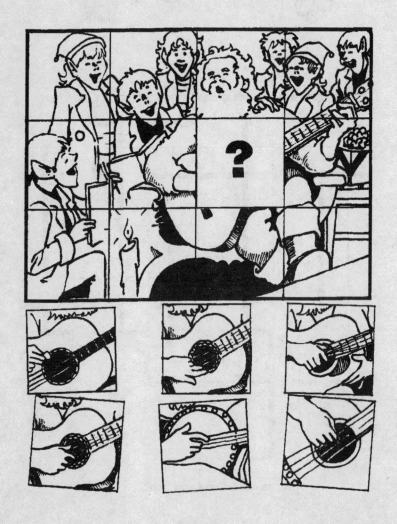

TOOLS OF THE TRADE

Match each character on the top with something related to his work on the bottom.

FIND THE TWINS #2

Find the two identical Santas.

ANSWERS

THE GAME OF THE NAME
Page 3

#6 has all the correct letters.

HOWDY!
Page 4

Halo

MAKING CONNECTIONS #1
Page 5

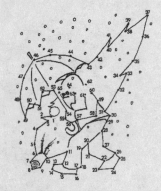

SCRAMBLER
Page 6

Why doesn't Saint Nicholas shave?

Every time he tries he nicks himself.

FIND THE TWINS #1
Page 7

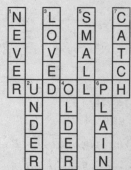

PUN FUN
Pages 8-9

Why does peanut butter hate Christmas?

Because 'tis the season to be jelly.

OPPOSITE DISTRACTION
Page 10

N		L		S		C
E		O		M		A
V		V		A		T
E		E		L		C
R	U	D	O	L	P	H
	N		L		L	A
	D		D		A	I
	E		E		I	N
	R		R		N	

Answer = *Rudolph*

SPELLING LINES #1
Page 11

MISSING PERSON
Pages 12-13

HA! HA!
Page 14

What goes "Ho, ho, ho, plop"?

Santa Claus laughing his head off.

A-MAZE #1
Page 15

SEASON'S GREETINGS
Pages 16-17

THE REAL SANTA
Page 18

He's a farmer who always says, "HOE HOE."

MISSING PIECE #1
Page 19

OH, DEER!
Page 20

CUPID
RUDOLPH
PRANCER
BLITZEN
DONNER
DASHER
VIXEN
COMET
DANCER

BOXED OUT #1
Page 21

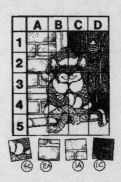

HOLIDAY FEAST
Pages 22-23

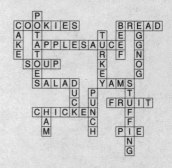

CROSS TALK
Pages 24-25

59

SITE-SEEING
Page 26

CONTINENT
     OCEAN
COUNTRY
  STATE
    HILL

    PRAIRIE
   MOUNTAIN
 ISLAND
  DESERT

Site = *North Pole*

HIDDEN WORDS
Page 27

RIDDLE READ
Page 28

In what movie does Santa meet aliens?

Claus Encounters

LOST AND FOUND
Pages 28-29

JUST JOKING
Pages 30-31

1. Green, blue, yellow, purple, red
2. Dare, care, mare, pare, fare
3. Boston, Richmond, Tulsa, Dallas, Reno
4. Sedan, convertible
5. Pizza, hamburger, sandwich
6. Kitchen, bedroom
7. Book, newspaper, diary

Riddle answer = *"It's Christmas, Eve."*

BOXED OUT #2
Pages 32-33

STORY LINE
Page 35

EAT IT!
Page 34

HAM
FARINA
SAUSAGE
YOGURT
BAGEL
EGGS
DOUGHNUT
OMELET
BACON
BISCUIT
OATMEAL

Riddle answer = *Mistletoast*

OOPS!
Page 36

TRAIN
SKATES
WAGON
CLOTHING
WATCH
RADIO

BOOK
BICYCLE
COMPUTER
TRUCK
PUZZLE

Riddle answer = *A Santa Klutz*

61

SPELLING LINES #2
Page 37

SOME SONG!
Pages 38-39

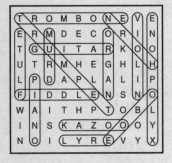

Riddle answer = *Deck the halls with poison ivy*

SOME PLACE!
Page 40

Answer = *Workshop*

TEST YOUR MEMORY
Pages 41-42

1. 8 o'clock
2. Yes
3. Four
4. A teddy bear
5. A pillow
6. Candles
7. No

REBUS
Page 42

GIRL - RL + FAN - AN + HAT - HA + SUN - UN = GIFTS

SOME DIFFERENCE
Page 43

62

A-MAZE #2
Page 44

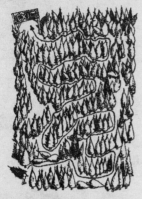

SIGN OF THE TIMES
Page 45

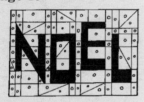

'TIS THE SEASON
Pages 46-47

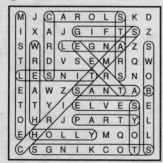

DRAW IT!
Pages 48-49

MRS. CLAUS
Page 50

MARBLE	M	BLARE
SEASON	A	NOSES
DANCER	R	CANED
CHEERY	Y	CHEER
CAROLS	C	SOLAR
DASHER	H	READS
WINTER	R	TWINE
SISTER	I	RESTS
FEASTS	S	FATES
TINSEL	T	LINES
MOTHER	M	OTHER
WREATH	A	THREW
SNOWED	S	OWNED

Riddle answer = *Mary Christmas*

**MAKING
CONNECTIONS #2**
Page 51

MISSING PIECE #2
Page 54

TOOLS OF THE TRADE
Page 55

HOLIDAY FILL
Pages 52-53

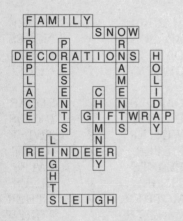

FIND THE TWINS #2
Page 56